ENVIRONMENT, TOOLS & MAN

T0346167

THE ORNAMENT

ENVIRONMENT, TOOLS & MAN

An Inaugural Lecture

BY

D. A. E. GARROD

*Disney Professor of Archaeology in
the University of Cambridge*

CAMBRIDGE
AT THE UNIVERSITY PRESS
1946

CAMBRIDGE
UNIVERSITY PRESS

University Printing House, Cambridge CB2 8BS, United Kingdom

Published in the United States of America by Cambridge University Press, New York

Cambridge University Press is part of the University of Cambridge.

It furthers the University's mission by disseminating knowledge in the pursuit of
education, learning and research at the highest international levels of excellence.

www.cambridge.org
Information on this title: www.cambridge.org/9781107641327

First published 1946
Re-issued 2014

A catalogue record for this publication is available from the British Library

ISBN 978-1-107-64132-7 Paperback

ENVIRONMENT,
TOOLS & MAN

ONE of my predecessors in this Chair, Professor Churchill Babington, in an Introductory Lecture delivered before the University of Cambridge in 1865, said that 'Archaeology...concerns itself with every kind of monument which the ravages of time have spared', and he rejoiced that 'the Disney Professor's choice is as wide as the world itself, so far as it concerns its archaeology. There is no country, there is no period about which he may not lecture, if he feels himself qualified to do so.' Sir Ellis Minns, in his Inaugural Lecture of nineteen years ago, illustrated this by enumerating the holders of the Chair; first a classical scholar, appointed by John Disney himself, John Howard Marsden, then Churchill Babington, a classic by formation, but with the widest interests, then Percy Gardner, a distinguished classical archaeologist, finally William Ridgeway, again an eminent classical scholar, but of whom his successor said that 'he embraced not only the archaeology, but the anthropology of all ages and races'. To these names I may now add that of my predecessor Sir Ellis Minns himself, the learned and brilliant historian of Scythians and Greeks, an expert palaeographer, who adds to a mastery of Russian a working knowledge of many other languages which the Postal Censorship officially designates as 'uncommon'.

To one whose claim to be an archaeologist is founded mainly on a knowledge of the Old Stone Age, such a list cannot but cause misgiving. It is true that Babington includes in the field of the archaeologist the cave-dwellers of the Périgord, then recently discovered, and the flint implements of Abbeville and St Acheul, which he doubted not 'were anterior by many ages to the Roman Empire'. Nevertheless, since Babington's time Palaeolithic studies have become so specialised, and have been brought into so close a relationship with the natural sciences, that their claim to be a province of archaeology in the accepted sense is sometimes regarded with suspicion by workers in a later field.

This is a mistake, but it is a mistake for which we prehistorians ourselves are partly responsible, and I think the time has come to take stock of our position. It is true, indeed, that as soon as we cross the dividing line of the Neolithic revolution, and enter that vast span of time which leads back to Man's first appearance on earth, we do, to a considerable extent, leave behind us the standards and the point of view of the archaeologist in the strict sense of the word. The prehistory of the Old Stone Age is far more closely bound up with certain branches of natural science—geology, palaeontology, palaeobotany—and the formation of a prehistorian in this sense calls for a scientific discipline to which the student of the later stages of Man's story is not normally submitted.

It is noteworthy that among those who have built up the study of Early Man nearly all the outstanding names belong to men who have approached it from one or other of the natural sciences. This recruitment is to be expected in a subject which touches those sciences at so many points, and it has been of the highest value in the development and systematisation of human palaeontology in the widest sense. On the strictly archaeological side, however—that is, in the study of the artefacts of fossil man—it has had certain results which are perhaps not quite so happy. It is time, I think, that these tendencies should be critically examined, and that we should ask ourselves whether they are not in part responsible for the present divorce between the student of the Old Stone Age and the archaeologist in the popular sense of the word.

The geologist or palaeontologist, having studied the natural formations—river terraces, moraines, loess—in which primitive artefacts are found, together with their associated fossil fauna, then proceeds to examine the artefacts themselves, and almost inevitably tends to apply to their classification the ideas and the vocabulary of the science in which he was trained. In other words he regards an artefact as a fossil, and is apt to treat it as subject to the laws of natural evolution, like any other fossil. Hence we too often find in Palaeolithic studies an exaggerated insistence on typology, and the improper application to the industries of the Old Stone Age of such terms as genus, species, hybridisation, cross-mutation and so on. This tendency is encouraged by the fact that the relics of early man are necessarily reduced to the virtually imperishable elements of his culture—that is, for the most part, to the stone implements which can have formed only a small part of his total heritage. In these conditions it is almost possible to lose sight of the fact that the chipped stones which he has bequeathed to us are indeed Man's handiwork; the more so since they are often found dispersed in river gravels and silts, divorced from all human context.

As I have said, I do not deny that the strict scientific approach, and the pre-occupation with classification which results from it, have been necessary and valuable for the systematisation of prehistory on the archaeological side, but it remains a one-sided approach, and we have now advanced nearly as far as it is possible to go in that direction. Stone implements, I repeat, are *artefacts*, imagined and made by Man, and variable at his free will; to ignore this element of incalculability is to force prehistory into a strait-jacket. In discussing a similar tendency to regard written history as 'a science and no more', G. M. Trevelyan[1] has recently said, 'The study of mankind does not resemble the study of the physical properties of atoms, or the life-history of animals.... Men are too complicated, too spiritual, too various, for scientific analysis.' And he adds, 'As Carlyle wrote long ago, "Every reunion of men, is it not a reunion of incalculable influences; every unit of it a microcosm of influences; of which how shall science calculate or prophesy?"'

The prehistorian would do well to ponder these

[1] *History and the Reader*, p. 12, Cambridge 1945.

words, bearing in mind, however, that in the study of Early Man the natural sciences in their rightful place remain indispensable, and form part of the essential structure of the subject. For example, without the chronological framework which geology and palaeontology alone can supply, the archaeologist can draw no valid conclusions and the whole pattern of development falls to pieces. Again, in the excavation of prehistoric sites, only a rigorously scientific and objective method of digging and observing and recording is admissible. My concern is that the natural sciences should not go on to monopolise a field which does not strictly belong to them—the study of Man as reflected in the work of his brain and his hands. In other words we must distinguish more clearly the true rôle of the separate disciplines involved, and apply to the various aspects of the subject the methods proper to each. This truth was perhaps more clearly perceived by some of the pioneers than by their successors. Gabriel de Mortillet, to whom we owe the first serious classification of the industries of the Old Stone Age, was at the same time genuinely interested in the human and social sides of pre-history, and Sollas, in his famous book, *Ancient Hunters*, set an example in the right approach which has never seriously been followed up. At Oxford, indeed, a small flame was kept burning for many years, and no pupil of R. R. Marett (as I am proud to be) could ever wholly forget that Man as a human being, and not Man as a fossil, is the true subject of the prehistorian.

In the present generation, reaction against the over-emphasis on classification and typology has already set in, and some of my younger colleagues (in particular Grahame Clark,[1] Hallam Movius,[2] A. J. H. Goodwin[3] among others) are developing an approach which is at the same time more realistic and more imaginative. If I sometimes seem to repeat what they have already written, I feel that no apology is needed; it simply means that we have been thinking on the same lines.

Let us now examine what, in fact, the natural sciences can properly give to the prehistorian, and how this information can most fruitfully be used by him. I have already spoken of the geochronological framework, which is of primary importance. In this field, many problems are still unsolved, and for a long time to come it will continue to absorb

[1] *Man and Nature in Prehistory*. Conference on the Problems and Prospects of European Archaeology, London 1944.
[2] *Early Man and Pleistocene Stratigraphy in Southern and Eastern Asia*, Cambridge, Mass. 1944.
[3] *Method in Prehistory*, Cape Town 1945.

a large part of the labour and interest devoted to Palaeolithic studies. Enough has been done, however, to provide the relative chronology which is indispensable to a study of the development of human cultures. Precisely the same evidence from geology and palaeontology which is utilised by the geochronologist gives us also the material for a reconstruction of Man's environment—geography, climate, the animal and to some extent the vegetable world—at any given stage of the Pleistocene, while the palaeontologist, in so far as the rather meagre skeletal material allows, can tell us what kind of human or near human being lived in that environment.

Having at his disposal the knowledge of which this is a brief summary, the prehistorian turns to the implements of stone and bone which in most cases form the only record of Man's presence on earth at any particular moment of the remote past. How much information, and what kind of information, can they be made to yield? Too often, as I have already suggested, it is thought sufficient to carry out a typological classification, sometimes very detailed, to relate the industry so studied to others already known, and to put a name to it—either an existing one, or newly coined, as need may be. If the material is sufficiently abundant, tables and graphs may be prepared, based on measurements of flaking-angles, depth of bulb of percussion, and so on. A minutely descriptive study of this kind can be a very imposing document, and is not without value, but a critical examination will show that it avoids the real issue; it is, fundamentally, a confession of defeat in face of the enormous gaps in our knowledge of Early Man. Of course, I have taken an extreme example, but we prehistorians are all more or less tarred with the same brush. I do not mean to suggest that we overlook entirely the sources we possess for a more complete approach to the subject, but I think it is fair to say that we practically never utilise them to the full. To establish a truly significant relation between the environment of Early Man and that small proportion of his handiwork which remains to us, requires a genuinely creative effort of thought and imagination; an effort difficult to make and all too easy to shirk.

Admitting that a typological classification of implements is a necessary preliminary to the study of any Stone Age culture, if only in order that those who have not direct access to it may use the material for comparison and interpretation, it remains then a part only of what must be attempted. So I repeat the question, how much information, and what kind of information, can these artefacts be made to yield? In the case of a late Palaeolithic culture like the Magdalenian, with its many weapons and chattels carved from bone and reindeer antler, and its marvellous cave art, the material relics alone can tell us a great deal about the men who made them, but the more ancient industries, which survive merely as a collection of chipped stones found dispersed in river sands and gravels, set a much more difficult problem. Here, the artefacts taken by themselves can, in fact, tell nothing but that they were made by man, and made in a certain fashion—in other words, as long as they are considered in isolation, the typological approach alone is possible. Our first effort then must be to reconstruct as completely as we can the physical environment of their makers. The world of Early Man has long since disappeared, its contours destroyed by erosion or buried in sand and silt, its animals vanished or transformed. It is our task, by a combined operation of knowledge and imagination, to make that world live again before our own eyes, and through it to interpret the tools which are the instruments of Man's response to his environment. At best, our knowledge of the earliest men will remain very imperfect, but I am confident that more can be achieved than has been attempted in the past, while the later Palaeolithic cultures, with their larger range of implements, their dwelling-sites, their food remains, their burials, and in some cases their artistic achievement, can be made to yield a very rich harvest.

For most stages of the Pleistocene, geology and palaeontology can give us a reasonably good account of geomorphology, climate, fauna and to a lesser extent flora for those regions of the Earth in which human relics have been found. When we have collated this information for a particular stage, we must ask ourselves what would be the *needs* of primitive man faced by such an environment. The answer will clearly depend to some extent on his place in the scale of physical evolution. Was he a man in every respect like ourselves, or one of those lowlier types, Sinanthropus, Pithecanthropus or Neandertal Man, whose demands on life, together with his skill in imagining and fashioning tools, must necessarily have been conditioned by the limitations of his imperfectly developed brain? The relative scarcity of skeletal remains of fossil man by comparison with his implements often makes it impossible to answer this question, but in many cases it can be answered, and its importance should not be overlooked.

In interpreting archaeological finds and in assessing the needs of early man, ethnographical comparisons, rightly used, can be of great value. This line of thought, so strikingly developed by Sollas in *Ancient Hunters*, for long lost favour, partly owing to the increasing pre-occupation with typology, partly because it had often been used uncritically and at random. It is misleading to seek individual comparisons with objects selected from present-day primitive cultures at varying levels of development, and flourishing under widely different conditions. The proper method is to compare the whole economy of a modern primitive people with the economy, as far as it is known, of a prehistoric people at approximately the same stage of social development, and living under similar conditions. Thus, Sollas' comparison of the Mousterian, the Aurignacian and the Magdalenian cultures with those of the Australian, the Bushman and the Eskimo respectively is, in the main, legitimate. Such a study will not only by direct comparison throw light on the imperishable relics which we actually possess, but will also, by bringing out the

16

needs of primitive man in face of a particular environment, and the means adopted to satisfy them, enable us to some extent to guess at what is missing from the prehistoric record.

For example, a hunter could not live unarmed, yet it has been noted that very early cultural traditions, such as those which in the Lower and Middle Pleistocene produced the so-called Hand-axe industries of the Western half of the Old World, and the Chopping-tool industries of the Eastern half, are lacking in any kind of stone artefact which could properly be called a weapon. Some pre-historians, beginning with Mortillet, have argued from this that the earliest men were pacifists and vegetarians, but the evidence is against them. We know, for instance, that one at any rate of the makers of chopping-tools, Sinanthropus Pekinensis, was not only a hunter of elephant, rhinoceros and deer, but probably also a head-hunter as well. Clearly he must have possessed at least some kind of spear, and since no possible spear-heads either of stone or bone have been found among his relics, this must have been made entirely of wood. A cave on Mount Carmel has actually furnished definite proof of the use of all-wood spears at a rather later date, by a people who had already begun to make flint points which could have served as spear-heads. One of the skeletons of the fossil man Palaeanthropus Palestinensis had a clean-cut hole passing through the head of the femur into the pelvis, and from this was obtained a plaster cast, reproducing the tip of a wooden spear which had been thrust into his vitals, and of which no other trace remained.

Now, although a spear is obviously a first necessity to any hunter of sizeable animals, even the simplest life demands a number of other chattels. The natives of Central Australia, among the most primitive of living peoples, inhabit a country of desert and scrub, with few large trees, yet even they, in their original state, possessed a fair range of wooden artefacts—shields, spear-throwers, boomerangs, clubs, vessels for food and drink. The makers of hand-axes, whose work in stone, though little varied, shows considerable skill and sense of form, may well have surpassed the Australian blackfellow in their handling and use of wood; the more lowly Sinanthropus probably fell below this standard, but even he was not lacking in dexterity, and a creature who lived by hunting and knew the use of fire must already have developed needs which could not be met by a handful of chipped pebbles and a pointed stick.

Wood, then, must have been a very important commodity to Early Man, and in estimating the extent to which it was likely to be used by a particular people, the presence or absence of trees in that region, at that time, as reflected in the contemporary fauna, becomes important. The man from Mount Carmel who was killed by a wooden spear was associated with animal remains which included a fair proportion of Persian fallow deer, a creature of woodland habitat which browses on deciduous trees and shrubs. As long as wood was obtainable, Man, although he utilised bone from his food remains, seems to have shirked the more difficult task of shaping and carving it, and it is not until the height of the fourth glaciation, among the Upper Palaeolithic peoples living north of latitude 42°, that is, in the relatively treeless tundra belt, that genuine artefacts of bone and antler begin to appear.

So far, I have suggested, in a general way, the part to be played by intelligent speculation, combined with various sources of evidence, in filling the gaps in our knowledge of the life and equipment of Early Man. When we come to examine the artefacts which we actually possess, we must see them also against the background of environment, bearing in mind their possible relation to the activities and purposes of those who devised them, and to all those other objects which have perished. This means that we must revert to the now rather discredited practice of trying to determine for what uses these stone implements were made. Nearly all known types have attached to them names dating from early days when prehistorians were interested in this question, but which are now admittedly treated as nothing more than convenient labels. Thus, we have points, borers, burins, and above all scrapers—a category which includes practically every worked flint that is not obviously something else. Now although these names are for the most part just typological labels, they still carry a suggestion of classification by function, and so rather block the way to further effort in this direction. As a beginning we might make a division into things which could be parts of weapons, and those which are clearly tools. Weapons are as a rule easier to classify; spear-heads, such as the beautifully worked leaf-shaped blades of the Solutrean and some at least of the Mousterian points, arrow-heads with one or more barbs, as in the Grimaldian and Upper Solutrean. It is much more difficult to identify tools according to function, and caution is needed, as many stone tools would be equally suitable for a number of purposes, although as intelligence and skill increased and Man's needs became more complex, implements became more varied and specialised. The Magdalenian craftsman, for example, must have had tools for carving bone and reindeer antler, and for engraving on these materials and on stone; as a dweller in an arctic climate he must also have made much greater use of animal skins, and therefore of tools for preparing and joining skins, than did the men of earlier times. Nevertheless the fundamental needs were probably much the same in nearly all Palaeolithic cultures; implements for digging up roots, for flaying and cutting up carcasses, for cutting and shaping wood. In view of this, and of the fact that the flaking of stone is subject to very definite limitations, the surprising thing is, not that Stone Age industries have so many features in common, but that even from the earliest times they differ so widely in many ways. An obvious example is that of the hand-axe and chopping-tool cultures already cited, but there are many others. Whatever the reasons—unequal physical and intellectual status, difference of raw material, difference of environment, or, above all, incalculability of the human mind—this variability of the tool in face of certain requirements that must have been more or less universal is a warning against dogmatism in classification by function. It might, indeed, be held to justify the typologists in throwing up the sponge when faced with this problem. Ethnography should help us here, and does to some extent, but unfortunately too little attention was paid, while there was still time, to ascertaining the precise functions of particular stone tools used by modern savages. How much might not have been learnt from the Tasmanians, to give only one example!

Nevertheless, I think there are various hopeful ways of approaching this problem, but I shall do no more than illustrate two possible methods, taking first the case of a culture with a very characteristic stone industry, which was carried by migration from one environment to another very different, and secondly, that of two distinct cultures at more or less the same stage of development, flourishing under similar conditions in adjoining regions, but showing marked differences.

The first case is that of the Aurignacian (or Middle Aurignacian), which is found all over an area extending from the eastern end of the Mediterranean through South-Eastern and Central Europe into Western Europe. It is believed that this culture spread from south-east to north-west, and in the course of this migration it passed from a warm climate, in which the Persian fallow deer still flourished, to a much colder environment, in which the reindeer was beginning to appear. The Aurignacian of Palestine and Syria from which worked bone is virtually absent is marked by a very high proportion of so-called burins and scrapers, which in fact, in spite of differences in size and shape and method of manufacture, are all tools displaying a very strong gouge-like working edge. The production of this type of edge seems to have been the chief pre-occupation of the Aurignacian flint-knappers; everything else is secondary, and, in particular, possible spear-heads or arrow-heads are rare. Spencer and Gillen have described the principal tool of the Central Australian tribes, in which a stone gouge of similar type, though usually less well-made, is fixed at the end of a spear-thrower, or a wooden rod, and is used in hollowing out and shaping vessels and shields, a method of working which gives a characteristic grooved surface to the wood. I suggest that the making of fairly large wooden objects, such as food vessels and shields, played a large part in the industrial tradition of the Aurignacian peoples of the Near East, while the rarity or absence of spear-heads in stone or bone shows that they still had weapons made entirely of wood. In Western Europe, the flint gouge remains a characteristic feature of this culture, and it should be noted that the contemporary fauna includes a fair proportion of red deer, a creature of woodland habitat, in addition to the reindeer, which presages the oncoming of arctic conditions. At the same time bone spear-heads and awls (the latter probably used for making holes in skins, for the change of climate must have made clothing essential) now form a regular part of the industry, and I am convinced that a more detailed analysis of the stone tools would reveal that here too there are innovations and changes which are significant in relation to the change of habitat.

As a caution I must add an indication that a stone tool originally made for one purpose may survive to be used for another. The so-called 'ordinary burin' (*burin en-bec-de-flûte*) is in fact a small straight-edged chisel. It is certain that in the Magdalenian this tool was used for cutting up reindeer antler by means of longitudinal grooves reaching into the spongy tissue, for these grooves show quite plainly the V-shaped form of the chisel edge. The ordinary burin is therefore regarded as specifically a tool for cutting reindeer antler by this method, yet it must originally have served a different purpose, for it occurs not only in earlier stages of the Western European succession, when reindeer antler was split by means of wedges, but also in cultures in which neither bone nor antler was ever worked at all.

My second case is one which should also, like the first, include the functional analysis of tools in relation to environment—in this case, diversity in face of similar conditions—but which at the same time opens a wider perspective. It is that of the Magdalenian and the slightly earlier Upper Palaeolithic cultures of Moravia and of South Russia, for which no generally accepted name has yet been found. Both flourished in conditions of great cold, but on the one hand we have cave-dwellers, with an economy based on the hunt of the reindeer, on the other a people living in huts on the open steppe, with an economy based on the hunt of the mammoth. Both were skilled in working and carving and engraving some form of bone, in the one case reindeer antler, in the other mammoth ivory, and in both the artistic sense was strongly developed, but expressed itself in strikingly different forms. There can be no doubt that the special qualities of antler and of ivory have played some part in determining the characteristic features of each artistic tradition, but the essential differences go deeper than this—they are the expression of those 'incalculable influences' which Carlyle said were found wherever men were found.

This brings me to my last point. In seeking to relate Man's handiwork to his environment, we must remember that we are dealing, not with a one-way process, but with an unceasing interaction. Some of our Soviet colleagues postulate a universal scheme of development from prehistoric to modern times, in which certain tools, made by a certain technique, appear inevitably at a given stage of society, the changes in social organisation themselves being determined by such factors as changes of climate, change of fauna, and so on. There is not much room here for Carlyle's 'incalculable influences'. Marxian prehistory is, of course, a special case, but over-emphasis on the determining influence of environment, and hence on the purely material factor in human development, is not confined to Russia. Even Gordon Childe, who gives due recognition to the action of the will in human history, can write,[1] 'Both evolution and cultural change may be regarded as adaptations to the environment', while in a very recent work Dr Frederick Zeuner[2] has said, 'Man is but too inclined to regard himself as the main figure on the earth's face. The real face of the earth is its landscape, determined by physiographical elements like elevation, relation to rivers, vegetation, animal life, and, dominating all, by the climate. It is the *environment* of Man. He depends on it in every respect, as regards food, clothing, housing; in short, the mode of life of a people is conditioned by its environment.'

'Man is but too inclined to regard himself as the main figure on the earth's face.' To that I answer, that he rightly so regards himself. I have said that Man's tools are the instruments of his response to the world in which he lives, but they are much more—they are the weapons of his conquest of that world. In the Old Stone Age we are assisting at the first, difficult stage of the struggle by which, in the end, through the power of his will and intelligence, Man has mastered his environment; this is the true drama of prehistory, the clue to its interpretation.

[1] *Man Makes Himself*, p. 23, London 1936.
[2] *Dating the Past*, p. 2, London 1946.

If Man, a comparatively small and puny mammal, had remained unarmed, he could have lived only by flight in a world which contained the elephant and the tiger. On the day when he first fashioned a rough wooden spear he gained the power, not only to stand and fight back, but in the end to turn the animal world to his own use. When he captured fire, and learned the way to kindle it himself, he obtained the means of cooking meat, and so of thriving on this food, for which his teeth were not by nature adapted. The capture of fire, which seems to be nearly as old as Man himself, led in the end to another triumph over environment, this one achieved only at a comparatively late date—at the earliest, towards the end of the third glaciation. For an immensely long period the hairless animal, Man, seems to have shifted back and forth with the other warmth-loving creatures as the ice-sheets advanced and retreated, but in the end, under what stimulus we do not know, with the help of fire and by the use of animal skins as clothing, he gained the power to live and finally to flourish under conditions of great cold. As Childe[1] has pointed out, the adaptation to a cold climate, which in the mammoth was a process of slow evolutionary

[1] *Man Makes Himself*, p. 21, London 1936.

change, in Man was a matter of deliberate choice, made possible, not by any change in his bodily structure, but by his own purposeful ingenuity and tenacity of will.

From the moment then that the geological record begins to carry alongside its fossils those roughly flaked stones which first announce the presence of the living, creative and unpredictable will of Man, history in the widest sense has begun. From the maker of hand-axes or choppers to the man of the twentieth century the human story is continuous and unbroken, and the student of the Old Stone Age who rightly comprehends his subject, equally with the Egyptologist or the expert in Greek sculpture, can claim the title of archaeologist. Human palaeontology, it is true, presents us with no visible single line of physical or social evolution. New types of Man and new industries constantly appear on the scene, to run a certain course, and then apparently to disappear. It is like a skein with a mass of broken ends, yet it is certain that somewhere within that skein, undetected so far, but present at every stage, is the thread which leads clear back from us here on earth to-day to the lowly forbears whose stone tools, harvested by the rivers of the world, are gathered into ancient gravels lying far above the present streams—the single unbroken thread which ties together the whole of Man's story. Not till that clue brings us at last to a being whom we can no longer recognise as human, may we leave the scientist in sole possession of the field.

www.ingramcontent.com/pod-product-compliance
Ingram Content Group UK Ltd.
Pitfield, Milton Keynes, MK11 3LW, UK
UKHW042141280225
455719UK00001B/26